THE WEALTH CODE

THE HIDDEN PSYCHOLOGY OF MONEY AND THE 90-DAY SYSTEM TO TURN FINANCIAL ANXIETY INTO INCOME, INCOME INTO ASSETS… AND ASSETS INTO POWER

INSPIRED LEGACY PRESS

EDGAR HERNÁNDEZ

INSPIRED
LEGACY PRESS

COPYRIGHT

Published by Inspired Legacy Press

Sparks, Nevada, USA

ISBN: 978-1-971513-42-3

Book Design and Layout: Inspired Legacy Press

Logo: Inspired Enterprises LLC

First Edition — 2025

Printed in the United States of America

EPIGRAPH

"Money does not respond to effort.
It responds to the mind that knows how to create it."

— Edgar Hernández · Inspired Legacy Press

DEDICATION

To those who feel deep within their soul
that they were born for something greater.
To those who refuse to accept a life limited
by fear, scarcity, or the rules of others.
To those who are ready to think differently,
act differently,
and build a reality most people
don't even dare to imagine.
This book is for those who have decided
to stop merely surviving...
and begin creating ***wealth, freedom, and power***
through their mind, their decisions, and their vision.
Because the world changes
every time someone discovers
the true code of wealth.
— Edgar Hernández · Inspired Legacy Press

ACKNOWLEDGMENTS

Acknowledgments

Writing about wealth is not simply about talking about money.

It is about **mindset, discipline, vision, and transformation.**

Throughout history, great thinkers, entrepreneurs, and creators have dedicated their lives to understanding the invisible laws that govern **success, abundance, and human progress.** Their ideas, discoveries, and philosophies have opened new paths for millions of people seeking to build a life greater than what the world once told them was possible.

To all those who have devoted their lives to studying, teaching, and expanding knowledge in **personal growth, mental development, financial strategy, and wealth creation**, I offer my deepest respect and gratitude. Their contributions have inspired entire generations to think differently and challenge the limits of what once seemed achievable.

I am also grateful to every reader who has chosen to hold this book in their hands. The simple act of seeking knowledge, questioning established beliefs, and aspiring to a life of greater freedom is already a powerful sign of **personal leadership.**

This book was written with a clear intention: **to offer a**

powerful perspective on money, the mind, and the creation of wealth—one that can transform the way people see their potential and their future.

If these pages awaken in you a new way of thinking, acting, and building your reality, then the purpose of this work will have been fulfilled.

— Edgar Hernández

CONTENTS

PROLOGUE

For generations, **money has been one of the most misunderstood subjects in human life.**

Most people spend years studying complex subjects, learning technical skills, and dedicating thousands of hours to mastering their work... yet almost no one receives a real education about **how money actually works**, how wealth is created, or how financial freedom is built.

Because of this, millions of people live trapped in a constant cycle of effort, worry, and financial limitation—even when they work hard and do everything they were told they were supposed to do.

It is **not a lack of talent.**

It is **not a lack of effort.**

It is **a lack of understanding.**

And yet, throughout history, there has always been a small group of people who seem to understand something different. People who are able to create wealth, expand opportunities, and build financial stability while others remain trapped in uncertainty.

The question that inevitably arises is simple:

What do they know that most people don't?

The answer is not found solely in financial strategies or economic formulas. The real difference begins in a much deeper place: **the way these individuals think, perceive, and make decisions about money.**

Before wealth ever appears in the physical world, it is first created in the mind.

The financial decisions we make, the risks we take, the opportunities we recognize, and the actions we execute are all shaped by an internal system of beliefs, perceptions, and habits that we rarely stop to question.

That invisible system is what this book calls **The Wealth Code.**

This code is not a magic formula or an unrealistic promise. It is a different way of understanding money, opportunity, and the personal power each individual possesses to create value, generate income, and build assets that can transform their future.

In the pages that follow, you will discover **how the psychology of money works**, why so many people remain trapped in financial anxiety, and how it is possible to transform that reality through a clear system of thinking and action.

Because **wealth is not an accident.**

It is the result of understanding certain principles, adopting certain mindsets, and executing certain decisions consistently.

And when a person begins to see money from this perspective, something begins to change.

Opportunities become more visible.

Decisions become more strategic.

And the relationship with money stops being driven by fear and begins to be guided by knowledge.

This book is an invitation to explore that shift.

An invitation to look at money from a different perspective—and to discover that behind what may appear to be a complex system reserved for a few, there are principles that **anyone can learn, apply, and master.**

The path to wealth begins long before financial results appear.

It begins **in the mind.**

And everything begins with understanding **the code.**

INTRODUCTION

The Real Problem with Money

For years, millions of people have lived with the same quiet feeling in the back of their minds.

They **work hard.**

They **put in the effort.**

They **try to do the right things.**

And yet, money always seems to slip through their hands.

It arrives... and disappears.

Unexpected expenses appear.

Opportunities seem to pass right in front of others—but never in front of them.

Meanwhile, they watch certain people who seem to be operating in an entirely different world. People who build businesses, multiply their income, create assets, and make financial decisions with a level of clarity that many find almost impossible to understand.

This inevitably raises a simple question:

What do they know that most people don't?

For a long time, we have been taught that wealth depends on factors such as luck, circumstances, or even the place where someone is born.

But when we look closely at those who consistently build wealth, we discover something far more interesting.

The difference does not begin with money.

It begins **in the mind.**

Before a person ever builds income, assets, or financial freedom, they first develop a different way of thinking about money, value, opportunity, and risk.

That way of thinking influences every decision they make.

It influences how they manage their money.

Which opportunities they recognize.

Which risks they choose to take.

And which actions they execute day after day.

Over time, those decisions produce **completely different financial outcomes.**

In other words, **wealth is not an accident.**

It is the result of a set of invisible principles that govern how people perceive and use money.

This set of principles is what we will call **The Wealth Code.**

Most people have never been exposed to this code.

Not because it is secret in the traditional sense, but because it simply is **not part of conventional education.** In school we learn mathematics, history, science, and many other important disciplines—but we rarely receive real education about how money works or how wealth is built in the modern world.

As a result, millions of people spend decades working

without ever fully understanding the financial game they are participating in every single day.

This book was written to change that.

In the pages ahead, you will discover how the **psychology of money** truly works, why so many people remain trapped in financial anxiety, and how it is possible to transform that reality through a clear system of thinking and action.

But there is something important you must understand from the beginning.

This book is not simply about **making more money.**

It is about something much deeper.

It is about developing a different way of thinking about money, value, and the personal power each individual has to build their own financial future.

Because when the mind changes, **decisions change.**

And when decisions change, **results inevitably begin to transform.**

For this reason, the book is structured around a **clear and progressive system.**

Throughout the chapters, you will discover **five fundamental codes** that explain how wealth is truly created.

The first code focuses on **the mind** and the invisible beliefs that shape our relationship with money.

The second focuses on **financial control**, an essential skill that separates those who live under constant financial pressure from those who build stability and clarity.

The third reveals how **income generation** truly works—and why some people seem to multiply opportunities while others remain trapped within the same limitations.

The fourth explores **asset creation**, the real engine that allows wealth to grow over time.

And finally, the fifth code presents a **practical 90-day**

system designed to help you apply these principles in a concrete way and begin transforming your financial reality.

Along this journey, you will discover something important:

Wealth is not a privilege reserved for a few.

It is a skill that can be learned.

A system that can be understood.

And a mindset that can be developed over time.

Everything begins with a simple decision.

The decision to question what you thought you knew about money.

And to open your mind to the possibility that behind the invisible rules of the financial world lies a code capable of transforming the way you build your life.

That code is about to be revealed.

Welcome to **The Wealth Code.**

PART I

CODE 1 — THE WEALTH MINDSET

Before a person builds wealth in the external world, something far more important happens in their **internal world.**

Every financial decision we make—from how we spend money to how we recognize opportunities—is influenced by an invisible set of **beliefs, perceptions, and mental habits** that formed long before we ever began thinking consciously about money.

That internal system acts like a filter.

It filters the opportunities we see.

It filters the risks we are willing to take.

And it filters the way we interpret **value, effort, and reward.**

Most people never question that system.

They simply repeat what they learned.

They learned to **work for money.**

They learned to believe that **money is difficult to earn.**

They learned that security comes from **stability, not expansion.**

Without realizing it, these ideas become a kind of **silent programming** that guides their decisions for years—even decades.

The problem is that many of these beliefs were created in contexts completely different from the world we live in today.

They were inherited from generations who lived in different economies, different opportunities, and very different realities.

Yet they continue to shape the way millions of people think about money.

For this reason, when some individuals begin to build wealth, it is not simply because they discovered a different financial strategy.

It is because they first developed **a different way of thinking.**

They began to see money as a **tool.**

They began to recognize opportunities where others saw only uncertainty.

And they began to make decisions based on **expansion rather than limitation.**

This mental shift is the first step toward understanding **The Wealth Code.**

Because wealth does not begin with a bank account.

It begins with **a different way of perceiving the world.**

In the chapters ahead, we will explore three fundamental elements that transform a person's relationship with money.

First, we will understand why most people never build wealth—even when they work hard.

Then we will examine the **invisible financial programming** that shapes our decisions without us even noticing.

And finally, we will discover how to develop an identity capable of **attracting, creating, and multiplying financial opportunities.**

This is **the first code.**

And as you will soon discover, when the mind changes, **everything else begins to change with it.**

1

WHY MOST PEOPLE WILL NEVER BUILD WEALTH

There is a belief deeply rooted in our society.

The idea that if a person works hard enough, sooner or later they will achieve financial stability—and perhaps even wealth.

From a young age, we hear phrases like:

"Work hard."

"Get a good job."

"Be responsible with your money."

In theory, this advice sounds reasonable. For generations, it has been presented as the natural path toward economic security.

Yet when we look at the real world honestly, a contradiction becomes difficult to ignore.

Millions of people work hard every single day...

and still live under constant financial pressure.

They wake up early.

They fulfill their responsibilities.

They try to manage their money carefully.

But the outcome rarely changes.

Money comes in... and goes out.

Debts appear.

Expenses grow.

And the feeling of financial stability always seems just a few steps away—but never fully within reach.

Meanwhile, there is another group of people who seem to operate under an entirely different set of rules.

People who **build businesses.**

Who **create assets.**

Who **multiply their income.**

And although they also work and face challenges, their relationship with money seems to move in a completely different direction.

The difference is not simply how hard they work.

It's how they think.

Because the fundamental difference between those who remain trapped in limited financial cycles and those who build wealth rarely begins with money.

It begins with **how they interpret the economic world.**

Most people were educated to participate in the economic system.

But very few were educated to understand **how that system actually works.**

They were taught to seek stability.

In exchange for time.

In exchange for effort.

In exchange for security.

But they were rarely taught how money is created, how value multiplies, or how assets are built to generate wealth over time.

As a result, millions of people spend decades **trading their time for limited income**, while others learn how to build systems that generate value even when they are not working directly.

This does not happen because some people are inherently smarter.

Or because they possess some extraordinary luck.

Or because they were born into perfect circumstances.

It happens because they developed **a different perspective about money.**

While most people think in terms of **income**, they think in terms of **assets.**

While most people seek **immediate security**, they build **long-term value.**

While most people see money as something earned through constant effort, they see it as something that can be **created, multiplied, and strategically directed.**

This shift in perspective **changes the entire game.**

And the most important part is this:

It is **not a talent reserved for a few.**

It is a way of thinking that can be learned.

But in order to learn it, we must first recognize something that many people find uncomfortable to accept:

The financial education most people received was never designed to teach them how to build wealth.

It was designed to teach them how to function within a specific economic system.

A system where **stability is prioritized over expansion.**

Where **security is prioritized over opportunity.**

And where money is viewed more as a reward for labor than as a **tool for creating value.**

When a person begins to question this programming, something interesting happens.

They start to see money from an entirely different perspective.

They begin to notice opportunities where they once saw only risk.

They begin to understand that wealth is not the result of a single event, but the result of **a series of strategic decisions accumulated over time.**

And most importantly:

They begin to realize that money does not respond only to effort.

It responds to **clarity of thought, strategy, and the ability to create value in the world.**

This is the first step toward deciphering **The Wealth Code.**

Before learning how to generate income, build assets, or develop financial systems, it is necessary to understand why so many people remain trapped in financial patterns that repeat themselves again and again.

Because once that pattern becomes visible, something changes.

The relationship with money stops feeling like a constant struggle.

And begins to feel like a **game of strategy, vision, and value creation.**

That mental shift is where everything begins.

And in the next chapter, we will explore one of the most powerful—and least visible—forces that shapes our relationship with money:

Invisible financial programming.

2

INVISIBLE FINANCIAL PROGRAMMING

Few people remember the exact moment when they began forming their ideas about money.

It didn't happen in a single conversation.

It wasn't the result of a single lesson.

It was a **quiet process** that began long before you had the ability to question it.

From childhood, all of us absorb messages about money.

Messages we hear **at home.**

At **school.**

In **family conversations.**

And through the culture that surrounds us.

Some phrases are repeated so often that they eventually become **unquestioned truths.**

"Money is hard to earn."

"Rich people must have taken advantage of someone."

"Money changes people."

"We weren't born to be rich."

You may not have heard those exact phrases.

But almost all of us have been exposed to **some version of them.**

And although these ideas are often expressed without bad intentions, they gradually begin to shape what we might call **a mental map of money.**

That mental map influences how we interpret financial opportunities.

It influences how much we believe we can earn.

It influences how much we believe we deserve.

And it even influences **how comfortable we feel having money.**

This phenomenon is what many psychologists refer to as **financial programming.**

It is the set of beliefs and perceptions that forms in our minds about money **long before we develop a conscious understanding of the economic world.**

And whether we realize it or not, that programming continues to influence our decisions for years.

It influences the careers we choose.

It influences whether we accept or reject opportunities.

It influences whether we believe something is **possible —or impossible—for us.**

The human mind operates largely through **patterns.**

When an idea is repeated enough times, the brain begins to treat it as a rule.

And once a rule becomes established in our mind, we tend to make decisions that **confirm it.**

For example, if a person deeply believes that money is scarce or difficult to obtain, they are far more likely to interpret opportunities with **fear or skepticism.**

If they believe stability is more important than expansion, they will likely avoid decisions that involve risk—even when those decisions could lead to growth.

Not because the person lacks intelligence or talent.

But because their mental system is trying to remain within the boundaries it considers **safe.**

This is one of the reasons why so many people feel financially stuck—even when they work hard.

They are not only struggling against external circumstances.

They are also operating within a **mental framework that limits what they believe is possible.**

But here is an important piece of news.

Mental programming is not permanent.

Beliefs can change.

Patterns can be rewritten.

And the way we interpret money can evolve.

The difference between those who remain trapped in limited financial cycles and those who begin to build wealth often starts with **a moment of awareness.**

A moment when a person realizes that many of the ideas they have accepted about money were **never actually examined.**

They were simply inherited.

And when that moment arrives, something begins to shift.

The rules stop feeling absolute.

Possibilities begin to expand.

And money stops appearing mysterious or inaccessible—it begins to look like **a system that can be understood.**

That is the moment when a person starts developing **a new relationship with money.**

A relationship based not on fear or limitation, but on **understanding.**

And once that understanding begins to grow, the next step becomes inevitable.

A person begins to change not only **what they think about money...**

but **who they believe they are capable of becoming.**

That is when the third fundamental element of the first code appears:

Financial identity.

Because in the end, wealth does not respond only to what we know.

It responds to **who we believe we are capable of becoming.**

3

THE IDENTITY THAT ATTRACTS MONEY

There is a question very few people ask themselves when they think about money.

Most people ask:

How can I make more money?

It is a logical question.

But it is also **an incomplete one.**

Because money rarely responds only to **what we do.**

It responds to **who we are when we make decisions.**

Two people can have access to the same opportunities, the same information, and even the same financial starting point.

Yet over time, their results can be completely different.

One may build stability, income, and assets.

The other may remain trapped in financial cycles that seem to repeat themselves again and again.

The difference is rarely intelligence, talent, or effort.

It lies in something much deeper.

Financial identity.

Financial identity is the way a person sees themselves in relation to money.

It is the set of beliefs, perceptions, and expectations that determine how we act when economic opportunities appear.

It influences decisions such as:

How much we believe we can earn.

How much money we believe we deserve.

What opportunities we believe are available to us.

And what kind of financial life we believe is possible to build.

Most people never reflect on their financial identity.

They simply act according to the story they have been telling themselves for years.

Stories like:

"I'm not good at business."

"Money has always been difficult for me."

"Big opportunities are for other people."

These phrases may seem harmless.

But when they are repeated for years, they become something more than thoughts.

They become **internal instructions.**

The human mind has an interesting characteristic.

It tends to behave in ways that remain consistent with the identity it believes it has.

If a person sees themselves as someone who always struggles with money, they will unconsciously make decisions that reinforce that narrative.

They may avoid certain risks.

They may underestimate their value.

Or they may even reject opportunities that could transform their financial situation.

Not because they want to fail.

But because their mind is trying to remain consistent with the story it believes about itself.

This phenomenon explains why many people experience temporary financial improvements only to return to their original situation.

Perhaps they receive a raise.

Perhaps they earn unexpected money.

Perhaps they experience a brief period of abundance.

But if their financial identity has not changed, over time their decisions tend to bring them back to the same level where they feel **"normal."**

For this reason, real financial transformation rarely begins with money.

It begins with **identity.**

People who consistently build wealth tend to develop a different identity.

They were not necessarily born with it.

They **developed it.**

They began to see themselves as **creators of value.**

As people capable of identifying opportunities.

As individuals capable of learning, adapting, and making strategic decisions.

That identity changes the way they see the world.

When an opportunity appears, they do not immediately think about why it might fail.

They think about **how it could work.**

When they face a financial challenge, they do not interpret it as proof of incapability.

They interpret it as **a problem that can be solved.**

And when they begin to generate results, they do not see them as luck.

They see them as evidence that they are **building something real.**

This shift in identity does not happen overnight.

It is a process.

A process that begins with a simple but powerful decision:

The decision to question the financial identity we have accepted for years.

To ask yourself:

Is the way I think about money actually helping me?

Are the beliefs I have about money truly mine...

or did I simply inherit them?

Does the story I tell myself about my financial possibilities reflect my real potential?

These questions can be uncomfortable.

But they can also be **deeply liberating.**

Because when a person begins to question their financial identity, something important happens.

The mind stops seeing the future as an automatic extension of the past.

It begins to see it as **a space of possibility.**

And that shift in perspective opens the door to new decisions.

Decisions that once seemed impossible.

Decisions that begin to build **a new narrative.**

The narrative of someone who is learning to understand money.

Someone who is developing financial skills.

Someone who is building a different relationship with opportunity.

In other words:

The narrative of someone who is beginning to **think like a wealth creator.**

And when that identity begins to strengthen, money stops feeling like a mystery.

It becomes **a consequence.**

A consequence of clearer decisions.

Of broader vision.

And of a mind that is no longer limited by the stories it once believed were permanent.

That is the true purpose of the first code.

It is not simply about learning new ideas about money.

It is about developing a mindset capable of seeing the financial world from an entirely different perspective.

Because when the mind changes, **decisions change.**

And when decisions change consistently, **results inevitably begin to transform.**

That is the moment when many people begin to notice something interesting.

Money stops feeling uncontrollable.

And begins to feel like something that can be **understood, directed, and multiplied.**

But for that transformation to continue, there is one fundamental skill that must be developed.

A skill that separates those who live under constant financial pressure from those who build economic stability and clarity.

That skill is **money control.**

PART II

CODE 2 — MONEY CONTROL

One of the greatest illusions about money is the belief that the main problem most people face is simply **earning more of it.**

At first glance, this idea seems logical.

If someone is experiencing financial difficulties, the most natural conclusion is that they simply need **more income.**

However, when we observe reality closely, we discover something surprising.

Millions of people increase their income throughout their lives...

and still continue to feel financial pressure.

They get a better job.

They receive a raise.

They earn more money than before.

But over time, something curious happens.

Their expenses increase as well.

New responsibilities appear.

Their lifestyle expands.

Financial obligations grow.

And the final result is that even though they earn more money than before, their sense of **financial control remains fragile.**

This happens because the real problem is rarely just the level of income.

The real problem is **the lack of control over the flow of money.**

The money that comes in.

The money that goes out.

And the decisions that connect the two.

Without control, even large incomes can disappear quickly.

With control, even moderate income can turn into **stability and growth.**

People who consistently build wealth develop a skill that often goes unnoticed.

They learn how to **direct money.**

Not simply how to earn it.

They understand that money behaves much like a current of energy that must be guided with intention.

If it moves without direction, it disperses.

If it is guided strategically, it can build something powerful over time.

For this reason, before discussing large investments, extraordinary opportunities, or advanced financial strategies, it is necessary to understand something fundamental:

Wealth begins with control.

Control over how money comes in.

Control over how it is used.

And control over how it is transformed into something capable of growing over time.

In the chapters ahead, we will explore **three essential elements** for developing this financial control.

First, we will examine one of the most common mistakes that keeps millions of people trapped in repetitive financial cycles.

Then we will explore the basic structure that allows money to be organized in a clear and strategic way.

And finally, we will examine how the flow of money actually works—and how to direct it intelligently to build **financial stability and growth.**

This is **the second code.**

The moment when money stops feeling unpredictable...

and begins to feel like something that can be **understood, organized, and directed with clarity.**

Because when a person learns to control money, something important changes.

Financial anxiety begins to fade.

Decisions become more intentional.

And the path toward building wealth begins to become visible.

That path begins by understanding the financial mistake that keeps millions of people trapped—**often without even realizing it.**

4

THE FINANCIAL MISTAKE THAT KEEPS PEOPLE TRAPPED

There is a financial phenomenon so common that most people experience it... **without even realizing it.**

It doesn't happen dramatically.

It doesn't happen overnight.

It happens slowly—almost invisibly.

And yet it is one of the most powerful reasons why millions of people work for decades **without ever building real wealth.**

This phenomenon is known as **lifestyle expansion.**

And it works in a very simple way.

When a person begins to earn more money, their lifestyle begins to expand at the same pace.

At first, the change seems completely reasonable.

Higher income allows certain improvements.

Perhaps a better car.

A more comfortable home.

More entertainment.

More conveniences.

None of this seems problematic.

In fact, in many cases it is completely natural to want to improve your quality of life when income increases.

The problem appears when this expansion happens **without strategy.**

Because when lifestyle grows at the same rate as income, something important never happens.

Money never gets the chance to become wealth.

It simply flows through a person's life.

Money comes in...

and money goes out.

Money comes in...

and money goes out.

And even though income may increase over time, the underlying financial structure remains essentially the same.

This pattern explains why many people with good incomes still live under **constant financial pressure.**

From the outside, their lives appear prosperous.

They have good jobs.

A comfortable lifestyle.

Certain luxuries.

But behind that appearance, their financial situation still depends entirely on **continuous income.**

If that income were to stop for an extended period of time, their financial stability could be seriously affected.

This happens because the money they earn is **not being transformed into assets that create wealth.**

Instead, it is primarily being transformed into **consumption.**

Modern culture constantly reinforces this pattern.

Advertising, social media, and social pressures send a subtle but powerful message:

As you earn more, **you should spend more.**

You should display more success.

You should continuously upgrade your lifestyle.

But people who truly build wealth understand something different.

They understand that there is a fundamental difference between **looking prosperous and being financially powerful.**

Looking prosperous means displaying visible signs of success.

Expensive cars.

Luxury clothing.

High spending.

Being financially powerful means something entirely different.

It means **owning assets.**

It means having **money working for you.**

It means your income does not depend solely on your time or direct effort.

This shift in perspective completely transforms a person's relationship with money.

Instead of seeing every increase in income as an opportunity to expand consumption, people who build wealth see it as an opportunity to **expand their base of assets.**

In other words, they direct money toward things that can **grow.**

Businesses.

Investments.

Productive assets.

This does not mean they never enjoy their money.

It means they understand **the right timing.**

First they build the foundation.

Then they enjoy the expansion.

Most people do the opposite.

They expand their lifestyle first.

And only afterward—if anything is left—do they think about building wealth.

The result is that there is often **nothing left to build something meaningful.**

Understanding this pattern is one of the most important moments in a person's financial transformation.

Because once it becomes visible, something changes.

Money stops being seen merely as a tool for consumption.

It begins to be seen as **a tool for building something greater than the present moment.**

And that shift in mindset opens the door to an even more important skill.

The ability to **organize money strategically.**

Because once we stop allowing money to flow without direction, an inevitable question appears:

How should money be organized to build stability, growth, and wealth?

The answer begins with something most people have never learned.

The structure of financial control.

5

THE FINANCIAL CONTROL STRUCTURE

One of the biggest mistakes many people make with money is not necessarily **spending too much.**

It is something far simpler.

They have no clear structure to direct it.

Most people handle money **reactively.**

Money comes in.

Bills are paid.

Expenses are covered.

Immediate needs are handled.

And whatever remains—if anything remains—is saved or used later.

This approach feels normal because it is what most people have seen their entire lives.

But it has an important flaw.

The money has no direction.

It simply responds to the circumstances of the moment.

People who build wealth rarely manage their money this way.

They use something far more powerful.

A structure.

A financial structure is a clear system that defines where money should go **before it even arrives.**

This changes the entire dynamic.

Instead of reacting to money, a person begins to **direct it with intention.**

Imagine money as if it were water.

If water flows without channels, it spreads everywhere.

But if well-designed channels exist, the water can be directed to specific places.

It can feed a system.

It can create movement.

It can generate growth.

Money works in a very similar way.

When there is no structure, money disperses into consumption, spontaneous spending, and impulsive decisions.

But when there is a clear structure, money begins to work **with purpose.**

One of the most effective and simple financial structures is based on dividing the flow of money into **three primary directions.**

The first direction is **stability.**

This portion of money is used to cover the essential needs of life.

Housing.

Food.

Basic services.

Financial responsibilities.

The goal of this portion is not growth, but **creating a solid foundation** that allows a person to operate with peace of mind.

The second direction is **expansion.**

This is where many people begin to separate themselves financially.

Instead of directing all their money toward consumption, a portion is directed toward activities that can increase their ability to generate income.

Education.

Skills.

Projects.

Business ideas.

This portion of money is not simply spent.

It is **invested in the future capacity to create value.**

The third direction is **wealth creation.**

This is the component many people never develop consistently.

It involves directing part of money toward **assets.**

Assets that can grow.

Assets that can generate income.

Assets that can multiply value over time.

When this structure begins to be applied consistently, something interesting happens.

Money stops being merely **a survival tool.**

It begins to become **a tool for building.**

Every dollar that comes in becomes an opportunity to strengthen stability, expand capabilities, and build wealth.

At first, this change may seem small.

But over time it creates an enormous difference.

Because when a person directs their money strategically for years, the result is not only stability.

It is **financial power.**

Not the power to spend more.

But the power to **choose.**

To choose how to use your time.

To choose which opportunities to pursue.

To choose how to build your future.

And everything begins with something as simple as **giving money a structure.**

However, even with a solid financial structure, there is still one key piece that determines a person's true financial growth.

That piece is understanding **how money moves through our decisions.**

Understanding how it flows.

How it multiplies.

And how it can be directed toward opportunities that generate **real growth.**

That will be the focus of the next chapter.

6

THE MONEY FLOW FORMULA

When most people think about money, they imagine it as something **static.**

A number in a bank account.

A monthly salary.

An amount that comes in and gets spent.

But in reality, money does not function in a static way.

Money behaves much more like a flow.

It is constantly moving.

It enters your life through certain activities.

It leaves your life through decisions.

And depending on how that movement is directed, it can either disappear quickly or begin to **multiply.**

Understanding this flow is one of the most important turning points in transforming your relationship with money.

Because when a person understands **how money moves**, they stop seeing it as something unpredictable.

They begin to see it as **a system.**

A system that can be observed, understood, and directed.

Imagine for a moment that all the money that passes through your life is like **a river.**

Every income stream is water flowing into that river.

Every expense is water flowing out.

If the water simply enters and exits without direction, the river never creates anything greater.

But if part of that flow is directed toward channels that feed reservoirs, crops, or productive systems, the same flow can begin to **generate growth.**

Money works exactly the same way.

Every person experiences a constant flow of money.

Some people generate small income streams.

Others generate large ones.

But the size of income does not always determine the final outcome.

What truly determines the result is **how the flow is directed.**

If all the money that comes in is immediately directed toward consumption, the flow is quickly exhausted.

But if part of that flow is directed toward assets that can grow over time, money begins to **change its behavior.**

It stops being something that simply passes through your life.

And begins to become something that **works inside your financial system.**

This is one of the most important differences between people who remain trapped in repetitive financial cycles and those who begin to build wealth.

The first group experiences money as something that constantly comes and goes.

The second group begins building structures where money **stays, grows, and produces more flow.**

When this happens, something interesting begins to occur.

Money starts generating money.

Income stops depending solely on time or direct effort.

And something emerges that many people pursue for years without fully understanding how it works:

financial leverage.

Leverage occurs when money, assets, or systems begin producing results **beyond the direct effort we invest.**

A business that continues generating income even when you are not actively working.

An investment that grows over time.

An asset that produces consistent cash flow.

All of this is the result of **directing the flow of money correctly.**

But this process does not begin with large investments or complex strategies.

It begins with a simple decision.

The decision to stop seeing money as something that is merely **earned and spent.**

And to begin seeing it as something that can be **directed, multiplied, and grown within a personal financial system.**

When a person adopts this perspective, their relationship with money changes profoundly.

Every income stream stops being simply money available to spend.

It becomes **a strategic opportunity.**

An opportunity to strengthen stability.

To expand capabilities.

And to feed assets that generate future growth.

That is the moment when money begins to behave differently.

Because **money responds to direction.**

And when it learns to flow toward assets, opportunities, and productive systems, something important begins to happen.

Money stops being merely a resource.

It becomes **a tool for building.**

This shift in perspective marks the conclusion of the second code.

Now the mind understands **money control.**

But there is still one essential piece required for the system to truly begin expanding.

Because before building assets, before creating strong financial systems, there is a skill that completely changes a person's economic trajectory:

the ability to generate income strategically.

That will be the focus of the next code.

PART III

CODE 3 — INCOME GENERATION

There is a fundamental difference between people who live with financial limitations and those who begin to build **real wealth.**

It is not only about how much money they earn.

It is about **how they see opportunities to generate it.**

Most people grow up believing that money primarily comes from a single source.

A job.

A salary.

A monthly income that arrives as the direct result of their time and effort.

For decades, this model has been presented as the natural path toward economic stability.

Work.

Receive a paycheck.

Manage that paycheck responsibly.

And while this model can provide basic stability, it also has an important limitation.

Income remains directly tied to time.

If time stops, the income stops as well.

People who begin to expand their financial reality discover something different.

They discover that money can be generated in many ways.

Through **skills.**

Through **ideas.**

Through **value created for other people.**

Instead of depending on a single source of income, they begin to develop a different mindset.

They start asking themselves:

How can I create more value?

What problems can I solve that other people are willing to pay to solve?

How can I transform my skills, ideas, or knowledge into economic opportunities?

When these questions become part of the way a person thinks, something important changes.

The economic world stops looking limited.

It begins to look **full of possibilities.**

Opportunities begin to appear in places where they were never seen before.

A skill can become a service.

Knowledge can become teaching.

An idea can become a project—or even a business.

Money stops being seen as something scarce that must be chased.

Instead, it begins to be seen as **a natural consequence of creating value in the world.**

This shift in perspective completely transforms a person's relationship with income.

Because when someone learns to generate value, **money begins to follow that value.**

Not magically.

But as the result of understanding **how economic exchange works.**

People pay for solutions.

They pay for convenience.

They pay for knowledge.

They pay for results.

And when someone develops the ability to offer those solutions consistently, money begins to move toward that person.

This is the point where many people begin to realize something powerful.

Income is not just something you receive.

It is something that can be **designed.**

It can be expanded.

It can be multiplied.

But for this to happen, it is necessary to understand how people who consistently generate income actually think.

Because those who create economic opportunities do not see money the same way as those who simply wait to receive it.

In the chapters ahead, we will explore **three fundamental ideas** that transform the way income is generated.

First, we will examine how people who create money strategically **think about opportunities.**

Then we will discover a key skill that has the power to **multiply the value a person can offer to the world.**

And finally, we will explore how to build a system that allows income to **expand progressively over time.**

This is **the third code.**

The moment when money stops feeling limited...

and begins to be seen as the natural result of understanding **how to create value, recognize opportunities, and act with vision.**

And everything begins with one fundamental question:

How do people who generate money actually think?

7

HOW MONEY CREATORS THINK

There is a quiet but powerful difference between those who constantly struggle with money and those who seem to discover economic opportunities almost anywhere.

That difference rarely lies in where they were born, their formal education, or even the resources they started with.

The difference begins somewhere much deeper.

The way they interpret the economic world.

Most people grow up seeing money as something that must be **obtained.**

Something that depends on finding the right job, waiting for an external opportunity, or having favorable circumstances.

From that perspective, money appears scarce.

Something that only shows up under certain conditions.

Something that must be **chased.**

But people who consistently generate money tend to see the world differently.

They don't begin by asking **where the money is.**

They begin by asking **where the value is.**

Because they understand a fundamental truth about how any economy works:

Money always follows value.

Every time someone pays for something, they do so because they believe what they receive has **more value than the money they give.**

People pay for solutions.

They pay for convenience.

They pay for knowledge.

They pay for results.

In other words, money constantly flows toward those who are capable of **creating value for others.**

When a person begins to understand this dynamic, the way they observe the world changes completely.

Opportunities stop appearing as rare events.

They begin to appear in unexpected places.

A problem becomes an opportunity for a solution.

A skill becomes an opportunity to serve.

Knowledge becomes an opportunity to teach.

The mind begins to operate differently.

Instead of thinking:

"Where can I find money?"

It begins to think:

"What value can I create?"

This shift in focus may seem simple, but its consequences are enormous.

Because when a person focuses on creating value, their relationship with money stops depending entirely on external circumstances.

It begins to depend on their ability to **observe, understand, and respond to the needs of the world around them.**

People who consistently generate income develop the habit of asking different questions.

Questions like:

What problem needs a solution?

What skill can I develop that would be valuable to others?

How can I improve something that already exists?

How can I make something simpler, faster, or more effective?

These questions open the door to new possibilities.

Because every time a problem finds a useful solution, **an economic opportunity appears.**

This is why many of the most successful business ideas did not come from inventing something entirely new.

They came from **improving what already existed.**

Making it more accessible.

More efficient.

More convenient.

The modern economy is filled with examples of this principle.

Companies that simplified processes.

Services that removed inconveniences.

Ideas that connected needs with solutions more effectively.

All of them were born from the same fundamental question:

Where can I create value?

When a person begins to train their mind to think this way, something interesting happens.

The economic world stops feeling limited.

It begins to look like a landscape filled with **problems waiting for solutions.**

And every problem can potentially become **an opportunity.**

However, recognizing opportunities is only part of the process.

For value to truly transform into income, something else must be developed.

A skill that multiplies the impact of any knowledge, talent, or idea.

A skill that allows ideas to be turned into **real results.**

That skill is the ability to **communicate and offer value clearly.**

Because in any economy, it is not enough to have something valuable.

You must also know how to **present it, share it, and connect it with the people who need it.**

That will be the focus of the next chapter.

8

THE SKILL THAT MULTIPLIES INCOME

If we observe people who generate large incomes across different industries, we notice something interesting.

Their professions can be completely different.

Some are entrepreneurs.

Others are investors.

Others create content, develop products, or build companies.

But when we look more closely, we find a skill that appears **again and again.**

A skill that connects all of these paths.

A skill that, when developed correctly, has the power to **multiply income in almost any field.**

That skill is **the ability to communicate value.**

In any economy, money moves toward those who solve problems and create value for others.

But there is an intermediate step that many people overlook.

It is not enough to **have something valuable.**

You must also know how to **present it, share it, and connect it with the people who need it.**

Otherwise, even a brilliant idea can remain invisible.

Imagine for a moment two people who possess **exactly the same skill.**

Both know how to do something useful.

Both can solve a real problem.

However, one of them knows how to clearly explain how their skill can help others, while the other struggles to communicate it.

Over time, their financial outcomes will likely be very different.

The first person will attract opportunities.

The second may remain unnoticed—even though they have the same talent.

This happens because the economic world operates through **exchanges of value.**

People pay when they clearly understand the benefit they will receive.

They pay when they perceive that something can improve their life, solve a problem, or help them achieve a desired result.

For this reason, the ability to communicate value becomes **an economic multiplier.**

It allows skills, ideas, and knowledge to transform into **real opportunities.**

But communicating value does not simply mean talking.

It means something deeper.

It means understanding **what other people truly need.**

Understanding the problems they face.

Understanding the results they want.

When a person understands this, the way they communicate changes completely.

They no longer speak only about **what they know how to do.**

They speak about **the results they can help create.**

This difference may seem subtle, but it has a massive impact.

Because people rarely buy skills.

They buy **results.**

They buy **solutions.**

They buy **transformations.**

A fitness coach does not sell exercises.

They sell **health, energy, and physical transformation.**

A consultant does not sell analysis.

They sell **clarity and strategy.**

An entrepreneur does not sell products.

They sell **solutions that make life easier for others.**

When a person learns to think in terms of value and results, their ability to generate income begins to expand.

They begin to see how their knowledge can become services.

How their skills can become opportunities.

How their ideas can become projects.

This process does not necessarily require starting with large resources.

Many of the most interesting economic opportunities begin with something far simpler:

A skill developed with dedication.

Knowledge that can be shared.

A solution that can be offered.

As a person develops this ability, something begins to change in the way they interact with the world.

They stop waiting for opportunities.

They begin **creating them.**

They start recognizing problems they can solve.

They begin seeing how their experience can help others.

And as these connections begin to form, money starts to appear as **a natural consequence.**

Not as something desperately chased.

But as the result of understanding **how value exchange works.**

However, even when a person develops the ability to generate income, there is still an important challenge.

If income depends entirely on time and direct effort, growth will always have a limit.

For this reason, people who truly expand their financial reality begin building something more.

They begin designing **systems that allow income to grow progressively.**

Systems where the value they create can reach more people.

Systems where opportunities can multiply.

That will be the focus of the next chapter.

9

THE FINANCIAL EXPANSION SYSTEM

At some point along the financial journey, many people discover something important.

Generating income is possible.

With effort, skills, and opportunities, it is possible to increase the amount of money that enters a person's life.

But after a certain point, a new question begins to emerge.

A question that separates those who simply improve their financial situation... from those who begin to build **real wealth.**

The question is this:

How can I make my income grow beyond my direct time and effort?

As long as income depends exclusively on the hours a person can work, growth will always have a limit.

The day has twenty-four hours.

Energy is finite.

Time is limited.

For this reason, even highly productive people can eventually reach a point where their ability to generate income begins to level off.

People who continue expanding their financial reality discover a different solution.

They begin to build **systems.**

A financial system is a structure that allows the value created by a person to reach more people, generate greater results, and produce income on a broader scale.

Instead of relying solely on direct effort, the system begins to **multiply impact.**

An entrepreneur who builds a business is creating a system.

An author who writes a book is creating a system that can reach thousands of readers.

An investor who places capital into productive assets is using a system that produces results over time.

In each of these cases, the same principle appears.

Value no longer depends solely on the person's direct presence.

Value begins to expand through structures that continue operating.

This shift in perspective is one of the most important moments in a person's financial evolution.

Because when someone begins thinking in terms of systems, their relationship with work changes.

The goal is no longer simply **to work more.**

The goal becomes **to create something that continues producing value over time.**

This does not mean eliminating effort entirely.

It means directing effort toward building something that has impact **beyond the present moment.**

Many people who have built significant wealth have spent years building systems.

Businesses.

Investments.

Projects.

Ideas that can grow and expand over time.

And once those systems begin to function, financial results stop depending exclusively on immediate effort.

They begin to emerge from **accumulated value.**

This is the point where many people begin experiencing something new.

Money stops feeling like something that must always be chased.

It begins to behave like something that **flows toward structures that create value.**

But here an important distinction appears.

Not all financial systems create real wealth.

Some simply generate income.

Others generate something far more powerful.

Assets.

An asset is anything that has the capacity to generate value or income over time.

It can be a business.

It can be an investment.

It can be property.

It can even be an idea that continues producing results.

People who build wealth begin directing more and more of their energy toward **creating and acquiring assets.**

Because they understand a fundamental truth.

Income can improve life.

But **assets build freedom.**

When assets begin generating a consistent flow of value, something extraordinary happens.

Money begins to work.

Not just the person.

This is the point where financial transformation begins to accelerate.

But for this process to develop in a solid and sustainable way, something even more important must be understood.

How to build wealth **in a structured way over the long term.**

That is the focus of the next code.

The code where money stops being simply **income...**

and begins to become **assets that build real wealth.**

Welcome to the next step of the system.

PART IV

CODE 4 — ASSET CREATION

There is a fundamental difference between **improving your financial life...**

and **building real wealth.**

Many people manage to improve their economic situation over time.

They find better jobs.

They increase their income.

They develop skills that allow them to earn more money.

However, even with higher income, many of those individuals still remain completely dependent on their ability to work.

If they stop working, the income stops.

And when the income stops, financial stability can quickly begin to weaken.

For this reason, although **income generation is a powerful skill**, by itself it is not enough to build lasting wealth.

Real wealth begins to form when a person starts creating something different.

Assets.

An asset is anything that has the ability to generate value, income, or growth over time.

Unlike direct labor, an asset can continue producing results even when a person is not constantly dedicating their time to it.

A business that generates income.

An investment that grows.

A property that produces rent.

A system that continues creating value.

All of these are examples of **assets.**

People who understand this principle begin to see money in a completely different way.

Money stops being something that is simply **earned and spent.**

It becomes a tool for **building assets that create more value over time.**

This is one of the main reasons why many people with high incomes never truly build wealth.

They generate money.

But they do not build enough assets.

Their income sustains their lifestyle, but it does not create a financial structure that continues to grow.

People who build wealth begin doing something different.

Every time they generate income, a portion of that money is directed toward **creating or acquiring assets.**

Over time, those assets begin to generate new income.

And that new income can then be directed toward **even more assets.**

This process creates a powerful effect.

Money begins to multiply.

Not instantly.

But gradually and consistently.

Over the years, this process can completely transform a person's financial reality.

Because there comes a point when assets begin generating enough value to support a person's lifestyle.

And when that happens, something emerges that many people spend their entire lives pursuing without fully understanding how it is built.

Financial freedom.

Financial freedom does not necessarily mean never working again.

It means having **the ability to choose.**

To choose how to use your time.

To choose which projects to pursue.

To choose which opportunities to follow.

When a person reaches this point, money stops being a constant source of worry.

It becomes a tool that allows life to be designed **with greater intention.**

But to reach that point, one key distinction must be understood.

The difference between income and assets.

That distinction is one of the most important ideas for anyone who truly wants to build wealth.

And it will be the focus of the next chapter.

10

INCOME VS. ASSETS: THE DIFFERENCE THAT CHANGES EVERYTHING

For most of a person's life, money is usually understood in a very simple way.

You earn money.

You pay expenses.

You try to save something for the future.

This model seems logical because it is what most people have seen since childhood.

However, when we begin to observe how wealth is truly built, a fundamental distinction appears—one that completely transforms the way money is understood.

The difference between income and assets.

At first glance, these two concepts may seem similar.

Both involve money.

Both are part of financial life.

But in reality, they represent **two completely different things.**

Income is the money that enters your life as a direct result of your work, your services, or your activities.

A salary is income.

A payment for a service is income.

The profits from a project are income.

Income is important because it allows us to cover needs, sustain daily life, and create opportunities for the future.

But income has one important characteristic.

It usually depends on **time, energy, or direct activity.**

If the activity stops, the income can also stop.

Assets, on the other hand, function in a completely different way.

An asset is something that has the ability to generate value or income over time—even when you are not actively working on it in that moment.

A property that produces rent is an asset.

An investment that grows over time is an asset.

A business that generates income even when you are not present every day is an asset.

A book that continues selling for years is an asset.

The key difference is that **assets continue producing value after the initial effort has been made.**

While income depends on continuous effort, assets have the ability to generate results **progressively over time.**

This distinction may seem simple.

But its implications are enormous.

Because when a person focuses only on income, their financial life becomes directly connected to their ability to work.

They will always need to generate new income to sustain their lifestyle.

People who begin to build wealth adopt a different strategy.

They understand that **income is important.**

But they see income as a **tool for building assets.**

In other words, they use income as raw material to create something bigger.

Every dollar earned becomes an opportunity to strengthen their financial structure.

Part of the money is used for living.

Another part is directed toward **building assets.**

Over time, those assets begin generating new income.

And that new income can be used again to acquire **more assets.**

This process creates something extremely powerful.

A cycle of growth.

At first, the progress may seem slow.

The first assets may generate small amounts of income.

But as the process continues, the system begins to expand.

More assets generate more income.

More income allows the creation of more assets.

And over time, the growth begins to accelerate.

This is the principle that has allowed many people to build wealth throughout history.

Not because they earned extraordinary amounts of money from the beginning.

But because they understood how to **transform income into assets.**

Once that process begins, money stops being something that is simply earned.

It becomes something that is **built.**

It is important to understand that building assets does not necessarily require starting with large investments.

Many assets begin in modest ways.

An idea that becomes a project.

Knowledge that becomes a product.

Income that is directed toward an investment.

What truly matters is not the initial size of the asset.

What matters is **the direction of the financial system.**

If money constantly flows toward consumption, it disappears.

If money progressively flows toward assets, it begins building something greater.

This shift in direction can completely transform a person's financial life.

Because when assets begin to grow, something interesting happens.

Money starts working.

And when money starts working, a person no longer depends exclusively on their own effort.

That is the moment when a personal financial system begins to gain real strength.

But an important question still remains.

How is wealth built consistently over time?

How does a collection of assets become a solid system that continues to grow?

That will be the focus of the next chapter.

11

HOW TO BUILD WEALTH THAT GROWS ON ITS OWN

When many people imagine wealth, they tend to picture **big moments.**

A massive business success.

An extraordinary investment.

A lucky break that suddenly transforms someone's financial life.

But when we look closely at how wealth has actually been built by most financially successful people, we find a very different story.

Wealth rarely appears overnight.

Wealth is **built.**

It is built through repeated decisions, intelligent structures, and time.

In reality, building wealth looks far more like **planting a tree** than winning a race.

When a person plants a seed, at first almost nothing seems to happen.

For days, weeks, or even months, the growth may be invisible.

But beneath the surface, something important is taking place.

Roots are forming.

The foundation is strengthening.

And when the tree finally begins to grow, it does so with a stability that allows it to continue expanding over time.

Wealth works in a very similar way.

The first assets a person builds may seem small.

A modest investment.

A project that begins generating income.

An idea that starts taking shape.

At first, the results may appear modest.

But what truly matters is not the initial size.

What matters is **the cumulative process** that begins to develop.

When assets generate value and that value is reinvested into new assets, the system begins to grow.

Each asset strengthens the structure.

Each additional stream of income creates new opportunities.

And over time, the growth begins to accelerate.

This phenomenon is known as **compound growth.**

Compound growth occurs when today's results become the foundation for even greater results tomorrow.

One asset generates income.

That income allows the creation of another asset.

That new asset produces more value.

And that value continues feeding the system.

At first, progress may feel slow.

But over time, the system begins to gain **remarkable momentum.**

What once seemed small begins to expand.

Opportunities begin to multiply.

And a personal financial system starts producing results that once seemed far away.

This is one of the most powerful principles in wealth creation.

It is not simply about **how much money you earn at a given moment.**

It is about **how you use that money to build something that continues to grow over time.**

People who understand this principle begin to think differently about money.

Every dollar earned stops being merely a resource to spend.

It becomes **an opportunity to strengthen the system.**

Every asset stops being viewed as an isolated result.

It becomes **a piece within a larger structure.**

Over time, this structure begins to produce something extraordinary.

Stability.

Not the fragile stability that depends on constant income.

But stability built on **assets that continue generating value.**

This is the true foundation of wealth.

It is not simply about having money.

It is about having **a system that continues producing value even when you are not actively working.**

When a person begins building this kind of system, their relationship with money changes profoundly.

Money stops feeling like something that must constantly be chased.

Instead, it begins to behave like something that **flows toward structures that produce growth.**

But for this process to work properly, one fundamental strategy must be applied.

A strategy that allows every asset, every dollar earned, and every financial decision to connect within a single system.

A strategy that transforms isolated efforts into **a coherent and powerful financial structure.**

That strategy is what we will explore in the next chapter.

12

THE STRATEGIC WEALTH ACCUMULATION SYSTEM

There is a very common misconception about wealth.

Many people believe that building wealth depends on making **one extraordinary decision.**

Finding the perfect investment.

Creating the ideal business.

Discovering the single opportunity that changes everything overnight.

But when we observe how wealth is actually built in the real world, a much more interesting reality appears.

Wealth is rarely the result of one single decision.

Wealth is the result of **many correct decisions accumulated over time.**

Decisions that, by themselves, may seem small.

But when they are repeated strategically over years, they begin to create **extraordinary results.**

This process can be understood as **strategic accumulation.**

Strategic accumulation occurs when a person consistently directs their resources—**time, money, knowledge,**

and opportunities—toward building assets and systems that generate value.

Instead of chasing immediate results, the person begins to think in terms of **cumulative growth.**

Every financial decision becomes a piece within a larger structure.

Every asset strengthens the system.

Every additional source of income creates new possibilities.

Over time, this accumulation produces something powerful.

A financial system that becomes stronger and more stable.

Imagine for a moment that every financial decision you make is like placing a brick.

A single brick may seem insignificant.

But when hundreds or thousands of bricks are placed with intention and consistency, they begin to form a structure.

A building.

A solid foundation.

Wealth works in a very similar way.

Every asset you build is a brick.

Every investment you make is a brick.

Every intelligent financial decision is a brick.

Over time, those bricks begin forming a financial structure capable of supporting **real growth.**

Most people, however, operate under a very different model.

Their financial decisions are reactive.

They respond to immediate circumstances.

They respond to the needs of the moment.

They respond to impulses of consumption.

The result is that money constantly flows in and out without contributing to a larger financial structure.

Strategic accumulation completely changes this dynamic.

When a person adopts this mindset, every financial decision is evaluated differently.

The question is no longer simply:

"Can I afford this?"

Instead, it becomes:

"Does this strengthen or weaken my financial system?"

This shift in perspective completely transforms the way money is used.

Decisions become more intentional.

Opportunities are analyzed with greater clarity.

And money increasingly flows toward structures that generate growth.

Over time, this approach produces a profound transformation.

The personal financial system begins to expand.

Assets begin to generate value.

Opportunities begin to multiply.

And something interesting starts to happen.

Financial progress stops feeling like a constant struggle.

It begins to feel like **a natural process of growth.**

But even with a solid system of strategic accumulation, one final piece still determines whether a person will truly apply these principles in their life.

Because understanding wealth is important.

But **applying it consistently** is what creates real results.

For that reason, the next code focuses on something essential.

A practical system.

A system designed to transform knowledge into action.

A system capable of beginning to change a person's financial reality in a matter of months.

That is the purpose of the final code.

The system that connects **mindset, control, income, and assets** into a clear process of execution.

Welcome to the final step.

PART V

CODE 5 — THE 90-DAY WEALTH SYSTEM

Throughout this book, we have explored a series of ideas that transform the way money is understood.

We have seen how **mindset influences the way we perceive opportunities.**

How **financial control allows us to direct money with intention.**

How **income generation emerges from creating value for others.**

And how **assets allow us to build wealth that grows over time.**

But there is a fundamental difference between **understanding a system** and **applying it.**

Many people discover powerful ideas about money.

They read books.

They listen to conferences.

They learn interesting concepts.

And yet, over time, their financial results remain exactly the same.

Not because the ideas are wrong.

But because **knowledge alone does not create results.**

Results appear when knowledge becomes **consistent action.**

For that reason, the final code of this book focuses on something extremely important.

Execution.

It is not about waiting for the perfect moment.

It is not about having every resource from the beginning.

It is about **beginning to apply the principles you have learned in a structured way.**

One of the most powerful ways to do this is through **defined periods of focused action.**

Periods in which a person directs their energy toward **clear financial objectives.**

One of the most effective frameworks for initiating this transformation is a **ninety-day period.**

Ninety days is enough time to create **real change.**

Enough time to develop **new financial habits.**

Enough time to begin **creating opportunities.**

And short enough to maintain **intense focus.**

During ninety days, a person can begin reorganizing their relationship with money.

They can take control of their finances.

They can begin expanding their ability to generate income.

And they can take the first steps toward **building assets.**

This period does not represent the end of the journey.

It represents **the beginning of the system.**

A system that can be repeated, improved, and expanded over time.

Because wealth does not appear as the result of a single action.

It appears when a person decides to **apply the right principles consistently.**

The next chapters are designed to help you transform what you have learned into **concrete actions.**

Actions that can begin transforming your financial reality.

Actions that can help you build **clarity, momentum, and direction.**

Because understanding **The Wealth Code** is the first step.

But **activating it in your life** is what truly changes the game.

And everything begins with a simple decision.

The decision to begin.

The next ninety days can become the moment when your relationship with money begins to transform.

And the first step begins now.

In the next chapter, we will explore the **first thirty days of the system—**

the stage where the foundation is built that will support everything else.

13

THE FIRST 30 DAYS: TOTAL FINANCIAL CONTROL

Every financial transformation begins with a specific moment.

A moment when a person stops **reacting to money...**

and begins **directing it.**

For years, many people live with a constant feeling of financial uncertainty.

They know money enters and leaves their lives, but they rarely have a clear picture of **how it truly moves.**

Expenses appear.

Responsibilities increase.

And although money constantly circulates, the personal financial system remains **unclear and undefined.**

For this reason, the first step of the ninety-day system has a clear objective:

to create total control over money.

Not control based on restriction or fear.

But control based on **clarity.**

Because when a person clearly sees how their money moves, something powerful happens.

Decisions begin to change.

Priorities become visible.

And money stops behaving like something unpredictable.

During the first thirty days, the primary goal is **not** to generate large income or build complex assets.

The goal is something more fundamental.

To create financial awareness.

The first step is to observe **the flow of money.**

How much money enters.

Where it comes from.

And where it goes.

Many people have never performed this exercise with real attention.

But when they do, they discover something revealing.

They discover **patterns.**

Patterns of spending.

Patterns of decisions.

Patterns that have influenced their financial reality for years.

This moment of observation is not meant to create guilt or judgment.

It is meant to create **clarity.**

Because only when something becomes visible can it begin to change.

The second step is to organize money according to the structure we explored earlier.

Each source of income begins to flow into three fundamental areas:

Stability.

Expansion.

Wealth Creation.

Stability ensures that essential needs are covered.

Expansion directs resources toward developing skills, opportunities, or projects that can generate more income.

And wealth creation begins building **assets that will produce value over time.**

During these first thirty days, many people experience something they have never felt before.

A sense of financial direction.

Money stops feeling like something that simply passes through their lives.

It begins to feel like **a tool that can be directed.**

The third step involves eliminating or reducing financial decisions that weaken the system.

This does not mean eliminating all enjoyment or comfort.

It means identifying expenses that do not contribute to growth or real well-being.

Small decisions that, accumulated over time, can weaken the financial system.

As these adjustments begin to occur, the system starts to strengthen.

Money begins to move with greater intention.

Priorities become clearer.

And the mind begins to experience something important.

Financial confidence.

Confidence not because everything has been solved.

But because **a system now exists.**

A system that allows decisions to be made with clarity.

By the end of the first thirty days, something fundamental will have changed.

Money will stop feeling like a chaotic force.

It will become a flow that can be **observed, understood, and directed.**

And once that control begins to establish itself, the next natural step appears.

Expansion.

Because once money is under control, the next question inevitably arises:

How can I generate more?

That will be the focus of the next chapter.

The second phase of the system.

Days 30 to 60.

14

DAYS 30–60: INCOME EXPANSION

Once a person has created clarity and control over their money, something interesting begins to happen.

The mind becomes **freer.**

Financial anxiety begins to decrease.

Decisions become more intentional.

And when this clarity appears, a new question naturally emerges.

How can I create more value... and as a result, more income?

During the first thirty days of the system, the objective was to build **control.**

Now, during this second thirty-day phase, the objective shifts.

The focus moves toward **income expansion.**

Many people spend years believing that their income is defined by external circumstances.

By their job.

By their industry.

By their current situation.

But when a person begins to think in terms of **value**, they discover something important.

Income is rarely limited only by where a person works.

It is far more connected to **the ability to create value for others.**

When someone learns to solve problems, facilitate results, or improve the lives of others, money begins to move toward that value.

For that reason, this second phase of the system focuses on developing **three fundamental areas.**

1. Skill Expansion

Every skill a person develops can become an economic opportunity.

A technical skill.

A creative skill.

A communication or leadership skill.

The modern world offers extraordinary opportunities for people who develop **useful abilities.**

Knowledge that can be shared.

Services that can be offered.

Solutions that can be created.

During these thirty days, the objective is to identify and strengthen skills that can generate value in the marketplace.

2. Opportunity Identification

Once the mind begins thinking in terms of value, the economic world begins to look different.

Problems become opportunities.

Needs become markets.

Ideas become projects.

Instead of waiting for opportunities, a person begins **actively searching for them.**

They begin asking questions such as:

What problem can I help solve?

What knowledge can I share?

What service can I offer that improves other people's lives?

These questions activate something powerful.

The mind begins to function like **an opportunity detector.**

3. Strategic Action

Ideas alone do not generate income.

Income appears when ideas are transformed into **action.**

During this phase, the objective is to begin applying skills and knowledge in the real world.

Small projects.

Initial services.

Ideas that begin to take shape.

Everything does not need to be perfect from the start.

In fact, many successful opportunities begin **in very simple ways.**

What matters most is **starting.**

Because every action generates learning.

Every attempt creates experience.

And every experience brings a person closer to larger opportunities.

As this process continues, something begins to shift.

The relationship with money stops feeling limited.

A person begins to realize that **they can create value.**

And when value begins to grow, income begins to expand as well.

By the end of this second thirty-day phase, the reader will have experienced something fundamental.

They will understand that money is not only something that is received.

It is something that can be created.

But one final step still remains in the system.

Because generating income is powerful.

However, to build **true wealth**, that income must be transformed into something more.

Assets.

The final phase of the system — **Days 60 to 90** — focuses precisely on that step.

The moment when money stops being only income...

and begins to become **real wealth.**

That will be the focus of the next chapter.

15

DAYS 60–90: ASSET BUILDING

After sixty days of focus and action, something important begins to change.

Your relationship with money is no longer the same.

The mind understands how it works.

Money begins to move with intention.

Income starts to expand.

But one final and crucial step remains to build **real wealth.**

Transforming income into assets.

This is the point where many people stop—often without realizing it.

They learn how to earn more money.

They learn how to organize their finances.

But they never complete the final step that allows the financial system to **grow on its own.**

That step is **consistently building assets.**

An asset is anything that has the ability to generate value or income over time.

An asset can take many forms.

A business that produces income.

An investment that grows over time.

A property that generates rent.

A product that continues selling.

A system that creates value for others.

The defining characteristic of an asset is simple.

It can produce results even when you are not actively working in that moment.

For this reason, during the final thirty days of the system, the objective shifts once again.

The focus is no longer only on **earning money.**

The focus becomes **building something that continues to produce value.**

During this period, every source of income begins to move with greater intention toward the creation or acquisition of assets.

It may be an initial investment.

It may be the development of a project that generates income.

It may be the beginning of a financial structure designed to grow over time.

At first, the assets may appear small.

But their importance does not lie in their initial size.

It lies in **the process they begin to activate.**

Each asset represents **a seed.**

A seed that, over time, can grow and produce new results.

When a person begins building assets consistently, something extraordinary happens.

Their personal financial system begins to **change its nature.**

Money stops depending exclusively on direct effort.

It begins to depend on **structures that generate value.**

As more assets are added to the system, growth begins to accelerate.

One asset generates income.

That income can be directed toward new assets.

And those new assets generate even more value.

This process creates something powerful.

A system that grows progressively over time.

This is the principle that has allowed many people to build wealth over the years.

Not necessarily because they earned extraordinary amounts of money from the beginning.

But because they learned to **direct money toward assets consistently.**

At the end of these ninety days, something fundamental will have changed.

Your relationship with money will no longer be the same.

Money will stop feeling like something that simply enters and leaves your life.

It will begin to feel like **a tool that can be directed, multiplied, and grown within a personal financial system.**

But even more important than the financial results, something deeper will have occurred.

A transformation in the way you think.

A transformation in the way you make decisions.

A transformation in the way you see opportunities.

Because when a person truly understands how money works, something changes forever.

Financial anxiety begins to disappear.

Clarity begins to emerge.

And the future stops feeling uncertain.

Instead, it begins to feel like something that can be **designed.**

That is the true purpose of this system.

Not only to generate money.

But to transform the way a person **builds their life.**

And when that transformation happens, a person no longer acts like someone who simply earns money.

They begin to act like someone who **creates wealth.**

And that identity is what we will explore in the final chapter.

16

THE WEALTH CREATOR IDENTITY

Throughout this book, we have explored ideas that profoundly transform the way a person can understand money.

We have seen that **wealth does not begin in a bank account.**

It begins **in the mind.**

It begins in the way a person perceives **value, opportunity, and their own ability to build something greater than their current circumstances.**

We have also seen that money is not simply something that appears or disappears at random.

It is **a tool.**

A tool that can be directed.

A tool that can be multiplied.

A tool that can become the foundation of **a strong financial system.**

But there is an even more important truth.

Wealth is not only the result of financial strategies.

Wealth is the result of **an identity.**

An identity that transforms the way a person **thinks, decides, and acts in the world.**

People who consistently build wealth did not necessarily begin with extraordinary financial knowledge.

What they developed was **a different way of seeing themselves.**

They began to see themselves as **creators of value.**

People capable of learning.

People capable of recognizing opportunities.

People capable of building something that did not exist before.

This identity changes the way a person moves through the world.

When a problem appears, it is not seen as an obstacle.

It is seen as **an opportunity for a solution.**

When an opportunity appears, it is not seen as distant or inaccessible.

It is seen as something that can be **explored.**

When money appears, it is not simply viewed as something to spend.

It is seen as **a tool for building something greater.**

Over time, this way of thinking completely transforms a person's financial life.

Decisions begin to align with **a larger vision.**

Income begins to flow toward assets.

Assets begin to generate new opportunities.

And gradually, the system begins to grow.

But perhaps the most important transformation does not happen in the money.

It happens **in the mind.**

A person stops feeling trapped by external circumstances.

They begin to feel capable of **designing their future.**

And when this transformation occurs, something interesting happens.

Wealth stops appearing like a distant destination.

It begins to look like **a natural consequence of correct decisions repeated over time.**

Money begins to flow toward structures that generate value.

Opportunities begin to multiply.

And life begins to move in a completely different direction.

This is the true meaning of understanding **The Wealth Code.**

It is not simply about learning how to earn more money.

It is about understanding **how the system works.**

It is about developing the mindset, the control, the ability to generate income, and the skill to build assets.

But above all, it is about developing **an identity.**

The identity of someone who does not simply participate in the economy...

but **creates value within it.**

Someone who does not simply earn money...

but **builds wealth.**

That is the moment when everything begins to change.

Because when a person adopts this identity, their decisions begin to align with a greater vision.

Every opportunity is evaluated with greater clarity.

Every dollar is directed with greater intention.

And every asset becomes a piece within **a growing financial system.**

From that moment forward, money stops being a constant concern.

It begins to become **a tool for designing life with greater freedom.**

And that, in essence, is the ultimate purpose of this entire process.

It is not only about wealth.

It is about **freedom, vision, and the conscious creation of the future.**

Now the code is in your hands.

The question is no longer whether the system works.

The question is much simpler.

What will you begin to build starting today?

THE BEGINNING OF SOMETHING GREATER

Somewhere in the world, at this very moment, someone is making a decision that will completely change their financial life.

It is not a spectacular decision.

It is not a stroke of luck.

It is a **quiet decision.**

The decision to **think differently.**

The decision to stop seeing money as a mystery or an uncontrollable force.

The decision to understand that **wealth is not a privilege reserved for a few.**

It is the result of understanding certain rules—and applying them with clarity.

Throughout history, every generation has produced people who learned to see the economic world differently.

People who understood that **money follows value.**

That **assets create freedom.**

And that **time, when combined with intelligent decisions, can multiply results in extraordinary ways.**

These individuals did not necessarily begin with extraordinary advantages.

Many began exactly where millions of people begin every day.

With an idea.

A decision.

A new way of thinking.

From that moment forward, they began to **build.**

They learned.

They experimented.

They made imperfect decisions—but they kept moving forward.

Over time, those decisions began to accumulate.

An additional income stream.

An asset.

An opportunity.

Another intelligent decision.

And little by little, the system began to grow.

What initially seemed small began to expand.

Opportunities began to multiply.

And money stopped feeling like a constant struggle.

It began to behave like **a tool within a system that generated growth.**

This is the process that has transformed the financial lives of many people over the years.

Not because they discovered a secret formula.

But because they decided to **learn the rules of the economic game—and apply them consistently.**

Now **you know those rules.**

You understand the importance of mindset.

You understand the power of financial control.

You understand the ability to create value and generate income.

And you understand the fundamental difference between **income and assets.**

But most importantly, you now have something even more powerful.

A different perspective.

A new way of seeing money.

And when that perspective changes, the economic world begins to look different.

Opportunities become more visible.

Decisions become more strategic.

And the future stops feeling uncertain.

Instead, it begins to feel like something that **can be designed.**

Wealth is not a destination that appears overnight.

It is a **process.**

A process built from small decisions made with intention.

Each correct decision strengthens the system.

Each asset adds a new piece.

Each opportunity builds on accumulated momentum.

Over time, that process begins to create something extraordinary.

A financial life with direction.

A structure that generates value.

And the freedom to design the future with greater clarity.

But all of this begins with something extremely simple.

A decision.

The decision to apply what you have learned.

The decision to **build.**

Because now the knowledge is in your hands.

The code has been revealed.

And the next page of this story will not be written in this book.

It will be written **in your life.**

Everything begins with the first step.

And that step... **begins today.**

Before closing these pages, it is important to understand something fundamental.

Money is only one dimension of human development.

True transformation occurs when **the mind, the body, identity, and life vision evolve at the same time.**

For that reason, *The Wealth Code* is part of a broader collection of works designed to explore different dimensions of personal growth: the mind, the body, purpose, discipline, vision, and the conscious construction of an extraordinary life.

Each of these books explores a different dimension of human potential.

Together, they form a system of learning designed for those who wish to go beyond superficial improvements and build **real, deep, and lasting transformation.**

If this book awakened a new way of thinking about money and opportunity within you, I invite you to continue exploring the rest of the works in this collection.

Because when knowledge expands across multiple dimensions of life, something extraordinary begins to happen.

Your relationship with money does not simply change.

Your way of thinking, acting, and building your future transforms.

And when that transformation occurs, the true power of knowledge begins to reveal itself.

MEET THE AUTHOR: THE FOUNDER OF INSPIRED LEGACY PRESS

Edgar Hernández is an author, speaker, and architect of human transformation. He is the founder of **Inspired Legacy Press**, an independent publishing imprint through which he leads a global movement dedicated to the mastery and evolution of human potential.

His work integrates **philosophy, science, and behavioral psychology** with emotional intelligence, neuro-biohacking, performance biology, longevity science, high-level habits, and systematic physical development to cultivate **mental clarity, inner strength, and unbreakable discipline.**

He is the creator of the **Inspired Legacy Framework**, a system of human transformation built upon four dimensions: **identity, body, wealth, and spirit.**

This framework is designed for individuals who choose to forge character, master their vital energy, expand their awareness, and build a life defined by real results rather than temporary motivation.

Through his books and teachings, he maintains a central conviction:

Those who master their mind, their emotions, and their habits... master their destiny.

This book forms part of an **Editorial System** conceived for the integral transformation of the individual.

A system built upon principles, structure, and long-term vision, where each work fulfills a precise role within a greater whole: cultivating **mental clarity, self-discipline, inner strength, and a conscious identity** capable of sustaining real results across the four dimensions of human development—**identity, body, wealth, and spirit.**

The purpose of the **Inspired Editorial System** is to refine judgment, elevate thinking, and forge character.

Each book is a pillar.

Each concept is a tool for real life.

This system is intended for those who understand that **personal growth is not a trend, but a deliberate and structured practice**—that freedom is built through knowledge, decision, and coherence—and that every true legacy begins in **the architecture of the mind.**

This is not self-help.

This is human architecture.

Master your identity.

Strengthen your body.

Multiply your wealth.

Expand your spirit.

Build power.

Build freedom.

Build legacy.

Welcome to the Inspired Universe.

instagram.com/edgarhernandezofficial

facebook.com/EdgarHernandezOfficial

youtube.com/@EdgarHernandezOfficial

Made in United States
Troutdale, OR
11/03/2026

56852546R00069